Home Maintenance LOG BOOK

This Log Book Belongs to

....

MAINTENANCE FOR

DETAILS

DATE _______________________________

PHONE _______________________________

SKETCH DETAIL _______________________________

SYSTEM APPLIANCE _______________________________

PROBLEM _______________________________

PREPARATION

HOW WAS IT RESOLVED?

Home Maintenance Log

MAINTENANCE FOR

DETAILS

DATE ______________________________

PHONE ______________________________

SKETCH DETAIL ______________________________

SYSTEM APPLIANCE ______________________________

____

PROBLEM ______________________________

____

____

____

PREPARATION

HOW WAS IT RESOLVED?

MAINTENANCE FOR

DETAILS

DATE

PHONE

SKETCH DETAIL

SYSTEM APPLIANCE

PROBLEM

PREPARATION

HOW WAS IT RESOLVED?

MAINTENANCE FOR

DETAILS

DATE _______________________

PHONE _______________________

SKETCH DETAIL _______________________

SYSTEM APPLIANCE _______________________

PROBLEM _______________________

PREPARATION

HOW WAS IT RESOLVED?

Home Maintenance Log

MAINTENANCE FOR

DETAILS

DATE ___________________________

PHONE __________________________

SKETCH DETAIL __________________

SYSTEM APPLIANCE ______________
____

PROBLEM _______________________
____
____
____

PREPARATION

HOW WAS IT RESOLVED?

Home Maintenance Log

MAINTENANCE FOR

DETAILS

DATE _______________________________

PHONE _______________________________

SKETCH DETAIL _______________________________

SYSTEM APPLIANCE _______________________________

____

PROBLEM _______________________________

____
____
____
____

PREPARATION

HOW WAS IT RESOLVED?

MAINTENANCE FOR

DETAILS

DATE _______________________

PHONE _______________________

SKETCH DETAIL _______________________

SYSTEM APPLIANCE _______________________

____

PROBLEM _______________________

____

____

____

PREPARATION

HOW WAS IT RESOLVED?

MAINTENANCE FOR

DETAILS

DATE
PHONE
SKETCH DETAIL
SYSTEM APPLIANCE

PROBLEM

PREPARATION

HOW WAS IT RESOLVED?

MAINTENANCE FOR

DETAILS

DATE _______________________________

PHONE _______________________________

SKETCH DETAIL _______________________

SYSTEM APPLIANCE ___________________

____

PROBLEM _____________________________

____

____

____

____

PREPARATION

HOW WAS IT RESOLVED?

MAINTENANCE FOR

DETAILS

DATE _______________________________

PHONE _______________________________

SKETCH DETAIL _______________________

SYSTEM APPLIANCE ___________________

____

PROBLEM _____________________________

____

____

____

____

PREPARATION

HOW WAS IT RESOLVED?

Home Maintenance Log

MAINTENANCE FOR

DETAILS

DATE

PHONE

SKETCH DETAIL

SYSTEM APPLIANCE

PROBLEM

PREPARATION

HOW WAS IT RESOLVED?

Home Maintenance Log

MAINTENANCE FOR

DETAILS

DATE ______________________________________

PHONE ____________________________________

SKETCH DETAIL ___________________________

SYSTEM APPLIANCE _______________________

____

PROBLEM _________________________________

____

____

____

____

PREPARATION

HOW WAS IT RESOLVED?

MAINTENANCE FOR

DETAILS

DATE ___________________________________

PHONE __________________________________

SKETCH DETAIL __________________________

SYSTEM APPLIANCE ______________________

____

PROBLEM ________________________________

____

____

____

____

PREPARATION

HOW WAS IT RESOLVED?

MAINTENANCE FOR

DETAILS

DATE ______________________________

PHONE ______________________________

SKETCH DETAIL ______________________________

SYSTEM APPLIANCE ______________________________

____

PROBLEM ______________________________

____

____

____

PREPARATION

HOW WAS IT RESOLVED?

Home Maintenance Log

MAINTENANCE FOR

DETAILS

DATE ____

PHONE ____

SKETCH DETAIL __________________________________

SYSTEM APPLIANCE _______________________________

____

PROBLEM ____

____

____

____

PREPARATION

HOW WAS IT RESOLVED?

MAINTENANCE FOR

DETAILS

DATE ____

PHONE _______________________________________

SKETCH DETAIL ________________________________

SYSTEM APPLIANCE _____________________________

____

PROBLEM _____________________________________

____

____

____

____

PREPARATION

HOW WAS IT RESOLVED?

MAINTENANCE FOR

DETAILS

DATE

PHONE

SKETCH DETAIL

SYSTEM APPLIANCE

PROBLEM

PREPARATION

HOW WAS IT RESOLVED?

Home Maintenance Log

MAINTENANCE FOR

DETAILS

DATE __________________________

PHONE _________________________

SKETCH DETAIL _________________

SYSTEM APPLIANCE ______________

____

PROBLEM _______________________

____

____

____

PREPARATION

HOW WAS IT RESOLVED?

Home Maintenance Log

MAINTENANCE FOR

DETAILS

DATE _______________________

PHONE _______________________

SKETCH DETAIL _______________________

SYSTEM APPLIANCE _______________________

____

PROBLEM _______________________

____

____

____

____

PREPARATION

HOW WAS IT RESOLVED?

Home Maintenance Log

MAINTENANCE FOR

DETAILS

DATE ________________________________

PHONE ________________________________

SKETCH DETAIL ________________________

SYSTEM APPLIANCE ______________________

____

PROBLEM ______________________________

____

____

____

____

PREPARATION

HOW WAS IT RESOLVED?

MAINTENANCE FOR

DETAILS

DATE ____________________________

PHONE ____________________________

SKETCH DETAIL ____________________________

SYSTEM APPLIANCE ____________________________

____

PROBLEM ____________________________

____

____

____

PREPARATION

HOW WAS IT RESOLVED?

MAINTENANCE FOR

DETAILS

DATE ___________________________

PHONE __________________________

SKETCH DETAIL __________________

SYSTEM APPLIANCE _______________

PROBLEM ________________________

PREPARATION

HOW WAS IT RESOLVED?

Home Maintenance Log

MAINTENANCE FOR

DETAILS

DATE __________________________________

PHONE _________________________________

SKETCH DETAIL _________________________

SYSTEM APPLIANCE ______________________

____

PROBLEM _______________________________

____

____

____

PREPARATION

HOW WAS IT RESOLVED?

MAINTENANCE FOR

DETAILS

DATE ____

PHONE ____

SKETCH DETAIL __________________________________

SYSTEM APPLIANCE _______________________________

PROBLEM _______________________________________

PREPARATION

HOW WAS IT RESOLVED?

Home Maintenance Log

MAINTENANCE FOR

DETAILS

DATE _______________________________

PHONE _______________________________

SKETCH DETAIL _______________________________

SYSTEM APPLIANCE _______________________________

____

PROBLEM _______________________________

____

____

____

____

PREPARATION

HOW WAS IT RESOLVED?

Home Maintenance Log

MAINTENANCE FOR

DETAILS

DATE _______________________________________

PHONE ______________________________________

SKETCH DETAIL _____________________________

SYSTEM APPLIANCE _________________________

PROBLEM ___________________________________

____

____

____

____

PREPARATION

HOW WAS IT RESOLVED?

MAINTENANCE FOR

DETAILS

DATE ___________________________

PHONE ___________________________

SKETCH DETAIL ___________________

SYSTEM APPLIANCE _______________

____

PROBLEM _________________________

____

____

____

PREPARATION

HOW WAS IT RESOLVED?

MAINTENANCE FOR

DETAILS

DATE ______________________________

PHONE _____________________________

SKETCH DETAIL _____________________

SYSTEM APPLIANCE __________________

____

PROBLEM ___________________________

____

____

____

____

PREPARATION

HOW WAS IT RESOLVED?

MAINTENANCE FOR

DETAILS

DATE ______________________________

PHONE ______________________________

SKETCH DETAIL ______________________

SYSTEM APPLIANCE ____________________

____

PROBLEM ____________________________

____
____
____
____

PREPARATION

HOW WAS IT RESOLVED?

MAINTENANCE FOR

DETAILS

DATE ________________________________

PHONE ________________________________

SKETCH DETAIL ________________________

SYSTEM APPLIANCE ____________________

____

PROBLEM ______________________________

____

____

____

PREPARATION

HOW WAS IT RESOLVED?

MAINTENANCE FOR

DETAILS

DATE ________________________________

PHONE ________________________________

SKETCH DETAIL ________________________

SYSTEM APPLIANCE ____________________

PROBLEM _____________________________

PREPARATION

HOW WAS IT RESOLVED?

MAINTENANCE FOR

DETAILS

DATE ________________________

PHONE ________________________

SKETCH DETAIL ________________________

SYSTEM APPLIANCE ________________________

PROBLEM ________________________

PREPARATION

HOW WAS IT RESOLVED?

Home Maintenance Log

MAINTENANCE FOR

DETAILS

DATE

PHONE

SKETCH DETAIL

SYSTEM APPLIANCE

PROBLEM

PREPARATION

HOW WAS IT RESOLVED?

MAINTENANCE FOR

DETAILS

DATE ___________________________

PHONE __________________________

SKETCH DETAIL __________________

SYSTEM APPLIANCE ______________

____

PROBLEM _______________________

____

____

____

PREPARATION

HOW WAS IT RESOLVED?

MAINTENANCE FOR

DETAILS

DATE ________________________________

PHONE _______________________________

SKETCH DETAIL ________________________

SYSTEM APPLIANCE ____________________

____

PROBLEM _____________________________

____

____

____

____

PREPARATION

HOW WAS IT RESOLVED?

MAINTENANCE FOR

DETAILS

DATE ___________________________________

PHONE __________________________________

SKETCH DETAIL __________________________

SYSTEM APPLIANCE ______________________

PROBLEM _______________________________

PREPARATION

HOW WAS IT RESOLVED?

MAINTENANCE FOR

DETAILS

DATE _______________________________

PHONE ______________________________

SKETCH DETAIL ______________________

SYSTEM APPLIANCE __________________

____

PROBLEM ___________________________

____

____

____

PREPARATION

HOW WAS IT RESOLVED?

Home Maintenance Log

MAINTENANCE FOR

DETAILS

DATE ____

PHONE ____

SKETCH DETAIL __________________________________

SYSTEM APPLIANCE _______________________________

____

PROBLEM ____

____

____

____

PREPARATION

HOW WAS IT RESOLVED?

Home Maintenance Log

MAINTENANCE FOR

DETAILS

DATE _______________________________

PHONE _______________________________

SKETCH DETAIL _______________________________

SYSTEM APPLIANCE _______________________________

____

PROBLEM _______________________________

____

____

____

PREPARATION

HOW WAS IT RESOLVED?

Home Maintenance Log

MAINTENANCE FOR

DETAILS

DATE ______________________________

PHONE ______________________________

SKETCH DETAIL ______________________________

SYSTEM APPLIANCE ______________________________

____

PROBLEM ______________________________

____

____

____

PREPARATION

HOW WAS IT RESOLVED?

MAINTENANCE FOR

DETAILS

DATE ___________________________

PHONE __________________________

SKETCH DETAIL __________________

SYSTEM APPLIANCE _______________

____

PROBLEM _______________________

____

____

____

PREPARATION

HOW WAS IT RESOLVED?

Home Maintenance Log

MAINTENANCE FOR

DETAILS

DATE ___________________________

PHONE __________________________

SKETCH DETAIL __________________

SYSTEM APPLIANCE ______________

____

PROBLEM _______________________

____

____

____

____

PREPARATION

HOW WAS IT RESOLVED?

MAINTENANCE FOR

DETAILS

DATE _______________________________

PHONE _______________________________

SKETCH DETAIL _______________________________

SYSTEM APPLIANCE _______________________________

____

PROBLEM _______________________________

____

____

____

PREPARATION

HOW WAS IT RESOLVED?

MAINTENANCE FOR

DETAILS

DATE ___________________________

PHONE ___________________________

SKETCH DETAIL ___________________________

SYSTEM APPLIANCE ___________________________

____

PROBLEM ___________________________

____

____

____

PREPARATION

HOW WAS IT RESOLVED?

MAINTENANCE FOR

DETAILS

DATE ___________________________________
PHONE __________________________________
SKETCH DETAIL __________________________
SYSTEM APPLIANCE _______________________
____
PROBLEM ________________________________
____
____
____
____

PREPARATION

HOW WAS IT RESOLVED?

MAINTENANCE FOR

DETAILS

DATE ___________________________________

PHONE __________________________________

SKETCH DETAIL ___________________________

SYSTEM APPLIANCE _______________________

____

PROBLEM ________________________________

____

____

____

PREPARATION

HOW WAS IT RESOLVED?

MAINTENANCE FOR

DETAILS

DATE ______________________________
PHONE ____________________________
SKETCH DETAIL ___________________
SYSTEM APPLIANCE ______________
____
PROBLEM _________________________
____
____
____
____

PREPARATION

HOW WAS IT RESOLVED?

MAINTENANCE FOR

DETAILS

DATE ________________________________

PHONE ________________________________

SKETCH DETAIL ________________________________

SYSTEM APPLIANCE ________________________________

PROBLEM ________________________________

PREPARATION

HOW WAS IT RESOLVED?

MAINTENANCE FOR

DETAILS

DATE ___________________________________

PHONE __________________________________

SKETCH DETAIL ___________________________

SYSTEM APPLIANCE _______________________

____

PROBLEM ________________________________

____

____

____

PREPARATION

HOW WAS IT RESOLVED?

Home Maintenance Log

MAINTENANCE FOR

DETAILS

DATE ______________________________________
PHONE _____________________________________
SKETCH DETAIL ____________________________
SYSTEM APPLIANCE ________________________
____
PROBLEM __________________________________
____
____
____

PREPARATION

HOW WAS IT RESOLVED?

MAINTENANCE FOR

DETAILS

DATE ___________________________

PHONE ___________________________

SKETCH DETAIL ___________________

SYSTEM APPLIANCE ________________

____

PROBLEM _________________________

____

____

____

PREPARATION

HOW WAS IT RESOLVED?

Home Maintenance Log

MAINTENANCE FOR

DETAILS

DATE ______________________________

PHONE _____________________________

SKETCH DETAIL _____________________

SYSTEM APPLIANCE __________________

PROBLEM ___________________________

PREPARATION

HOW WAS IT RESOLVED?

Home Maintenance Log

MAINTENANCE FOR

DETAILS

DATE _______________________________

PHONE _______________________________

SKETCH DETAIL _______________________

SYSTEM APPLIANCE ___________________

____

PROBLEM _____________________________

____

____

____

PREPARATION

HOW WAS IT RESOLVED?

Home Maintenance Log

MAINTENANCE FOR

DETAILS

DATE _______________________________

PHONE _______________________________

SKETCH DETAIL _______________________________

SYSTEM APPLIANCE _______________________________

PROBLEM _______________________________

PREPARATION

HOW WAS IT RESOLVED?

Home Maintenance Log

MAINTENANCE FOR

DETAILS

DATE

PHONE

SKETCH DETAIL

SYSTEM APPLIANCE

PROBLEM

PREPARATION

HOW WAS IT RESOLVED?

Home Maintenance Log

MAINTENANCE FOR

DETAILS

DATE _______________________________________

PHONE ______________________________________

SKETCH DETAIL ______________________________

SYSTEM APPLIANCE ___________________________

____

PROBLEM ___________________________________

____

____

____

PREPARATION

HOW WAS IT RESOLVED?

Home Maintenance Log

MAINTENANCE FOR

DETAILS

DATE _______________________________

PHONE ______________________________

SKETCH DETAIL ______________________

SYSTEM APPLIANCE ___________________

____

PROBLEM ____________________________

____

____

PREPARATION

HOW WAS IT RESOLVED?

MAINTENANCE FOR

DETAILS

DATE ___________________________

PHONE __________________________

SKETCH DETAIL __________________

SYSTEM APPLIANCE ______________

PROBLEM _______________________

PREPARATION

HOW WAS IT RESOLVED?

MAINTENANCE FOR

DETAILS

DATE ___________________________

PHONE __________________________

SKETCH DETAIL ___________________

SYSTEM APPLIANCE _______________

____

PROBLEM ________________________

____

____

____

____

PREPARATION

HOW WAS IT RESOLVED?

MAINTENANCE FOR

DETAILS

DATE ____

PHONE ____

SKETCH DETAIL __________________________________

SYSTEM APPLIANCE _______________________________
____

PROBLEM ____
____
____
____

PREPARATION

HOW WAS IT RESOLVED?

MAINTENANCE FOR

DETAILS

DATE ___________________________

PHONE ___________________________

SKETCH DETAIL ___________________________

SYSTEM APPLIANCE ___________________________

____

PROBLEM ___________________________

____

____

____

PREPARATION

HOW WAS IT RESOLVED?

Home Maintenance Log

MAINTENANCE FOR

DETAILS

DATE ___________________________

PHONE ___________________________

SKETCH DETAIL ___________________________

SYSTEM APPLIANCE ___________________________

____

PROBLEM ___________________________

____

____

____

PREPARATION

HOW WAS IT RESOLVED?

Home Maintenance Log

MAINTENANCE FOR

DETAILS

DATE _______________________________

PHONE _______________________________

SKETCH DETAIL _______________________________

SYSTEM APPLIANCE _______________________________

____

PROBLEM _______________________________

____

____

____

PREPARATION

HOW WAS IT RESOLVED?

MAINTENANCE FOR

DETAILS

DATE ______________________________

PHONE ______________________________

SKETCH DETAIL ______________________

SYSTEM APPLIANCE __________________
____

PROBLEM ___________________________
____
____
____
____

PREPARATION

HOW WAS IT RESOLVED?

Home Maintenance Log

MAINTENANCE FOR

DETAILS

DATE _______________________________

PHONE _______________________________

SKETCH DETAIL _______________________________

SYSTEM APPLIANCE _______________________________

____

PROBLEM _______________________________

____

____

____

____

PREPARATION

HOW WAS IT RESOLVED?

MAINTENANCE FOR

DETAILS

DATE _______________________________

PHONE _______________________________

SKETCH DETAIL _______________________________

SYSTEM APPLIANCE _______________________________

PROBLEM _______________________________

PREPARATION

HOW WAS IT RESOLVED?

MAINTENANCE FOR

DETAILS

DATE ________________________________

PHONE ________________________________

SKETCH DETAIL ________________________

SYSTEM APPLIANCE _____________________

____

PROBLEM ______________________________

____

____

____

PREPARATION

HOW WAS IT RESOLVED?

Home Maintenance Log

MAINTENANCE FOR

DETAILS

DATE ___________________________________

PHONE __________________________________

SKETCH DETAIL __________________________

SYSTEM APPLIANCE _______________________

____

PROBLEM ________________________________

____

____

____

PREPARATION

HOW WAS IT RESOLVED?

MAINTENANCE FOR

DETAILS

DATE _______________________

PHONE _______________________

SKETCH DETAIL _______________________

SYSTEM APPLIANCE _______________________

PROBLEM _______________________

PREPARATION

HOW WAS IT RESOLVED?

MAINTENANCE FOR

DETAILS

DATE ______________________________

PHONE ______________________________

SKETCH DETAIL ______________________________

SYSTEM APPLIANCE ______________________________

____

PROBLEM ______________________________

____

____

____

PREPARATION

HOW WAS IT RESOLVED?

MAINTENANCE FOR

DETAILS

DATE _______________________________

PHONE _______________________________

SKETCH DETAIL _______________________________

SYSTEM APPLIANCE _______________________________

____

PROBLEM _______________________________

____

____

____

PREPARATION

HOW WAS IT RESOLVED?

Home Maintenance Log

MAINTENANCE FOR

DETAILS

DATE ______________________________________

PHONE ______________________________________

SKETCH DETAIL ______________________________________

SYSTEM APPLIANCE ______________________________________

PROBLEM ______________________________________

PREPARATION

HOW WAS IT RESOLVED?

MAINTENANCE FOR

DETAILS

DATE ______________________________

PHONE ______________________________

SKETCH DETAIL ______________________________

SYSTEM APPLIANCE ______________________________
____

PROBLEM ______________________________
____
____
____

PREPARATION

HOW WAS IT RESOLVED?

MAINTENANCE FOR

DETAILS

DATE _______________________________

PHONE _______________________________

SKETCH DETAIL _______________________________

SYSTEM APPLIANCE _______________________________

____

PROBLEM _______________________________

____

____

____

PREPARATION

HOW WAS IT RESOLVED?

MAINTENANCE FOR

DETAILS

DATE ___________________________

PHONE __________________________

SKETCH DETAIL ___________________

SYSTEM APPLIANCE _______________

____

PROBLEM _______________________

____

____

____

PREPARATION

HOW WAS IT RESOLVED?

Home Maintenance Log

MAINTENANCE FOR

DETAILS

DATE ______________________________

PHONE ______________________________

SKETCH DETAIL ______________________________

SYSTEM APPLIANCE ______________________________

____

PROBLEM ______________________________

____

____

____

PREPARATION

HOW WAS IT RESOLVED?

MAINTENANCE FOR

DETAILS

DATE _______________________________

PHONE _______________________________

SKETCH DETAIL _______________________________

SYSTEM APPLIANCE _______________________________

____

PROBLEM _______________________________

____

____

____

____

PREPARATION

HOW WAS IT RESOLVED?

Home Maintenance Log

MAINTENANCE FOR

DETAILS

DATE _______________________________

PHONE _______________________________

SKETCH DETAIL _______________________________

SYSTEM APPLIANCE _______________________________

____

PROBLEM _______________________________

____

____

____

PREPARATION

HOW WAS IT RESOLVED?

MAINTENANCE FOR

DETAILS

DATE _______________________________

PHONE _______________________________

SKETCH DETAIL _______________________

SYSTEM APPLIANCE ___________________

____

PROBLEM _____________________________

____

____

____

PREPARATION

HOW WAS IT RESOLVED?

MAINTENANCE FOR

DETAILS

DATE _______________________________

PHONE _______________________________

SKETCH DETAIL _______________________

SYSTEM APPLIANCE ___________________

PROBLEM _____________________________

PREPARATION

HOW WAS IT RESOLVED?

Home Maintenance Log

MAINTENANCE FOR

DETAILS

DATE _______________________________

PHONE _____________________________

SKETCH DETAIL _____________________

SYSTEM APPLIANCE _________________

____

PROBLEM ___________________________

____

____

____

PREPARATION

HOW WAS IT RESOLVED?

MAINTENANCE FOR

DETAILS

DATE _______________________________

PHONE _______________________________

SKETCH DETAIL _______________________________

SYSTEM APPLIANCE _______________________________

____

PROBLEM _______________________________

____

____

____

PREPARATION

HOW WAS IT RESOLVED?

Home Maintenance Log

MAINTENANCE FOR

DETAILS

DATE _______________________

PHONE ______________________

SKETCH DETAIL ______________

SYSTEM APPLIANCE ___________

PROBLEM ____________________

PREPARATION

HOW WAS IT RESOLVED?

Home Maintenance Log

MAINTENANCE FOR

DETAILS

DATE _________________________

PHONE _________________________

SKETCH DETAIL _________________________

SYSTEM APPLIANCE _________________________

____

PROBLEM _________________________

____

____

____

PREPARATION

HOW WAS IT RESOLVED?

Home Maintenance Log

MAINTENANCE FOR

DETAILS

DATE _________________________________

PHONE _______________________________

SKETCH DETAIL _______________________

SYSTEM APPLIANCE ____________________

____

PROBLEM _____________________________

____

____

____

PREPARATION

HOW WAS IT RESOLVED?

Home Maintenance Log

MAINTENANCE FOR

DETAILS

DATE ___________________________________

PHONE __________________________________

SKETCH DETAIL ___________________________

SYSTEM APPLIANCE ________________________

____

PROBLEM ________________________________

____

____

____

PREPARATION

HOW WAS IT RESOLVED?

Home Maintenance Log

MAINTENANCE FOR

DETAILS

DATE _______________________________

PHONE _______________________________

SKETCH DETAIL _______________________

SYSTEM APPLIANCE ____________________

____

PROBLEM _____________________________

____

____

____

PREPARATION

HOW WAS IT RESOLVED?

Home Maintenance Log

MAINTENANCE FOR

DETAILS

DATE ______________________________

PHONE ______________________________

SKETCH DETAIL ______________________________

SYSTEM APPLIANCE ______________________________

PROBLEM ______________________________

PREPARATION

HOW WAS IT RESOLVED?

Home Maintenance Log

MAINTENANCE FOR

DETAILS

DATE ___________________________

PHONE __________________________

SKETCH DETAIL __________________

SYSTEM APPLIANCE _______________

PROBLEM ________________________

PREPARATION

HOW WAS IT RESOLVED?

MAINTENANCE FOR

DETAILS

DATE _______________________________

PHONE _______________________________

SKETCH DETAIL _______________________

SYSTEM APPLIANCE ____________________

PROBLEM _____________________________

PREPARATION

HOW WAS IT RESOLVED?

MAINTENANCE FOR

DETAILS

DATE ___________________________________

PHONE __________________________________

SKETCH DETAIL __________________________

SYSTEM APPLIANCE _______________________

____

PROBLEM ________________________________

____

____

____

PREPARATION

HOW WAS IT RESOLVED?

Home Maintenance Log

MAINTENANCE FOR

DETAILS

DATE ______________________________

PHONE ______________________________

SKETCH DETAIL ______________________________

SYSTEM APPLIANCE ______________________________

____

PROBLEM ______________________________

____

____

____

PREPARATION

HOW WAS IT RESOLVED?

Home Maintenance Log

MAINTENANCE FOR

DETAILS

DATE ___________________________________

PHONE __________________________________

SKETCH DETAIL __________________________

SYSTEM APPLIANCE _______________________

____

PROBLEM ________________________________

____

____

____

PREPARATION

HOW WAS IT RESOLVED?

Home Maintenance Log

MAINTENANCE FOR

DETAILS

DATE ______________________________

PHONE ______________________________

SKETCH DETAIL ______________________________

SYSTEM APPLIANCE ______________________________

PROBLEM ______________________________

PREPARATION

HOW WAS IT RESOLVED?

MAINTENANCE FOR

DETAILS

DATE _______________________________

PHONE _______________________________

SKETCH DETAIL _______________________________

SYSTEM APPLIANCE _______________________________

PROBLEM _______________________________

PREPARATION

HOW WAS IT RESOLVED?

MAINTENANCE FOR

DETAILS

DATE

PHONE

SKETCH DETAIL

SYSTEM APPLIANCE

PROBLEM

PREPARATION

HOW WAS IT RESOLVED?

MAINTENANCE FOR

DETAILS

DATE _______________________________

PHONE _______________________________

SKETCH DETAIL _______________________

SYSTEM APPLIANCE ____________________

____

PROBLEM _____________________________

____

____

____

PREPARATION

HOW WAS IT RESOLVED?

MAINTENANCE FOR

DETAILS

DATE ______________________________

PHONE ______________________________

SKETCH DETAIL ______________________________

SYSTEM APPLIANCE ______________________________

____

PROBLEM ______________________________

____

____

____

PREPARATION

HOW WAS IT RESOLVED?

Home Maintenance Log

MAINTENANCE FOR

DETAILS

DATE ______________________________________

PHONE _____________________________________

SKETCH DETAIL _____________________________

SYSTEM APPLIANCE _________________________

____

PROBLEM __________________________________

____

____

____

PREPARATION

HOW WAS IT RESOLVED?

Home Maintenance Log

MAINTENANCE FOR

DETAILS

DATE _______________________

PHONE _______________________

SKETCH DETAIL _______________________

SYSTEM APPLIANCE _______________________

PROBLEM _______________________

PREPARATION

HOW WAS IT RESOLVED?

Home Maintenance Log

MAINTENANCE FOR

DETAILS

DATE ______________________________________

PHONE _____________________________________

SKETCH DETAIL _____________________________

SYSTEM APPLIANCE _________________________

____

PROBLEM ___________________________________

____

____

____

____

PREPARATION

HOW WAS IT RESOLVED?

Home Maintenance Log

MAINTENANCE FOR

DETAILS

DATE _______________________________

PHONE _______________________________

SKETCH DETAIL _______________________________

SYSTEM APPLIANCE _______________________________

PROBLEM _______________________________

PREPARATION

HOW WAS IT RESOLVED?

Home Maintenance Log

MAINTENANCE FOR

DETAILS

DATE _______________________

PHONE _______________________

SKETCH DETAIL _______________________

SYSTEM APPLIANCE _______________________

PROBLEM _______________________

PREPARATION

HOW WAS IT RESOLVED?

Home Maintenance Log

MAINTENANCE FOR

DETAILS

DATE _______________________________

PHONE _______________________________

SKETCH DETAIL _______________________________

SYSTEM APPLIANCE _______________________________

____

PROBLEM _______________________________

____

____

____

____

PREPARATION

HOW WAS IT RESOLVED?

Home Maintenance Log

MAINTENANCE FOR

DETAILS

DATE ____

PHONE _______________________________________

SKETCH DETAIL _______________________________

SYSTEM APPLIANCE ____________________________

____

PROBLEM _____________________________________

____

____

____

PREPARATION

HOW WAS IT RESOLVED?

MAINTENANCE FOR

DETAILS

DATE ________________________________

PHONE _______________________________

SKETCH DETAIL _______________________

SYSTEM APPLIANCE ____________________

____

PROBLEM _____________________________

____

____

____

____

PREPARATION

HOW WAS IT RESOLVED?

MAINTENANCE FOR

DETAILS

DATE

PHONE

SKETCH DETAIL

SYSTEM APPLIANCE

PROBLEM

PREPARATION

HOW WAS IT RESOLVED?

MAINTENANCE FOR

DETAILS

DATE ______________________________________

PHONE ______________________________________

SKETCH DETAIL ______________________________

SYSTEM APPLIANCE ___________________________

____

PROBLEM ____________________________________

____

____

____

____

PREPARATION

HOW WAS IT RESOLVED?

Home Maintenance Log

MAINTENANCE FOR

DETAILS

DATE _______________________________

PHONE _______________________________

SKETCH DETAIL _______________________________

SYSTEM APPLIANCE _______________________________

____

PROBLEM _______________________________

____

____

____

PREPARATION

HOW WAS IT RESOLVED?

Home Maintenance Log

MAINTENANCE FOR

DETAILS

DATE ________________________

PHONE ________________________

SKETCH DETAIL ________________________

SYSTEM APPLIANCE ________________________

PROBLEM ________________________

PREPARATION

HOW WAS IT RESOLVED?

MAINTENANCE FOR

DETAILS

DATE ______________________________

PHONE ______________________________

SKETCH DETAIL ______________________

SYSTEM APPLIANCE __________________
____

PROBLEM ____________________________
____
____
____
____

PREPARATION

HOW WAS IT RESOLVED?

Home Maintenance Log

MAINTENANCE FOR

DETAILS

DATE

PHONE

SKETCH DETAIL

SYSTEM APPLIANCE

PROBLEM

PREPARATION

HOW WAS IT RESOLVED?

MAINTENANCE FOR

DETAILS

DATE _______________________________________

PHONE ______________________________________

SKETCH DETAIL ______________________________

SYSTEM APPLIANCE __________________________

PROBLEM ___________________________________

PREPARATION

HOW WAS IT RESOLVED?

MAINTENANCE FOR

DETAILS

DATE ____________________

PHONE ____________________

SKETCH DETAIL ____________________

SYSTEM APPLIANCE ____________________

____

PROBLEM ____________________

____

____

____

PREPARATION

HOW WAS IT RESOLVED?

MAINTENANCE FOR

DETAILS

DATE _______________________________

PHONE _______________________________

SKETCH DETAIL _______________________________

SYSTEM APPLIANCE _______________________________

____

PROBLEM _______________________________

____

____

____

____

PREPARATION

HOW WAS IT RESOLVED?

Home Maintenance Log

MAINTENANCE FOR

DETAILS

DATE _______________________________

PHONE _______________________________

SKETCH DETAIL _______________________________

SYSTEM APPLIANCE _______________________________

PROBLEM _______________________________

PREPARATION

HOW WAS IT RESOLVED?

Home Maintenance Log

MAINTENANCE FOR

DETAILS

DATE ___________________________

PHONE __________________________

SKETCH DETAIL __________________

SYSTEM APPLIANCE _______________

____

PROBLEM ________________________

____

____

____

____

PREPARATION

HOW WAS IT RESOLVED?

Home Maintenance Log

MAINTENANCE FOR

DETAILS

DATE

PHONE

SKETCH DETAIL

SYSTEM APPLIANCE

PROBLEM

PREPARATION

HOW WAS IT RESOLVED?

MAINTENANCE FOR

DETAILS

DATE __________________________

PHONE __________________________

SKETCH DETAIL __________________________

SYSTEM APPLIANCE __________________________

____

PROBLEM __________________________

____

____

____

PREPARATION

HOW WAS IT RESOLVED?